Compiled by Lin Fang

CHINESE NEW YEAR PAINTINGS

CHINA INTERCONTINENTAL PRESS

图书在版编目（CIP）数据

中国年画：英文／林方编著；刘浚译.—北京：五洲传播出版社，2007.12
（中国民间工艺品丛书）
ISBN 978-7-5085-1209-9

Ⅰ.中…　Ⅱ.①林…②刘…　Ⅲ.年画－简介－中国－英文
Ⅳ.J218.3

中国版本图书馆 CIP 数据核字（2007）第 171795 号

策　　划：荆孝敏
编　　者：林　方
翻　　译：刘　浚
特约编辑：吕　蕾
责任编辑：王　莉
装帧设计：缪　惟　汪俊宇

中国年画

出版发行：五洲传播出版社
社　　址：北京市海淀区莲花池东路北小马厂 6 号华天大厦
邮政编码：100038
电　　话：010-58891281
传　　真：010-58891281
制版单位：北京锦绣圣艺文化发展有限公司
印　　刷：北京郎翔印刷有限公司
开　　本：889x1194　1/24
印　　张：4.5
版　　次：2008 年 10 月第 2 版　2008 年 10 月第 1 次印刷
书　　号：ISBN 978-7-5085-1209-9
定　　价：68.00 元

Preface

New Year paintings (*nian hua*) belong to the Chinese folk paintings created for the traditional Spring Festival. Drawn by folk artists, the paintings are made in special studios and sold on rural fairs before the Spring Festival, which generally falls in January or February. With bright and contrasting colors and auspicious symbolic patterns, the paintings have enjoyed great popularity among local Chinese and overseas visitors. Before the early 20th century, it was customary for Chinese to buy New Year Paintings upon each Spring Festival and put them at home, hoping for good luck and happiness in the coming year.

New Year paintings appeared very early in history. Experts have found written records in the Han Dynasty (206 BC-AD 220) about a pair of brothers named Shen Tu and Yu Lei who were believed to be door guardians. Paintings about them were called "*men hua*" - door paintings, from which the New Year paintings have developed. Even today, paintings on the door are still an important genre of the New Year paintings. But it wasn't until the Qing Dynasty (1644-1911) that the term "*nian hua*" - New Year paintings - formally appeared to refer to such seasonal paintings that embodied people's good wishes. The earliest written record containing "*nian hua*" appeared in the book *Amusing Rural Talks* (*Xiang Yan Jie Yi*) written by Li Guangting, a native of Baodi in today's Hebei Province who lived during the rule of Emperor Daoguang (1782-1850) in the Qing Dynasty. Among the ten must-dos before the Spring Festival, Li says that "people give their houses a thorough cleaning, then put on New Year paintings, which are about children playing".

As they were part of the interior decorations for the nation's main festival, there were different rules for paintings aimed at different places. They were so well designed that in the past, almost every prominent corner in a house was taken up by one such painting.

New Year paintings on the door are called "*men hua*". On the front door, the guardians are usually fully armed generals whom people believe can keep all evils away. On doors inside the house, the guardians are generally imperial ministers or chubby children, who are believed to bring good luck. Inside the main hall, New Year paintings on the most important wall are called "*zhong tang*" or "*gong qian*" - the former is a large vertical drawing and the latter is a horizontal art work. Some people also prefer two vertical paintings of the same size, which are called "*dui ping*". The paintings in the main hall generally portray the three immortals that represent good luck, high official ranking and longevity. The paintings could also depict a scene from a folk opera or some local scenery or folk customs. Besides these, there are many paintings to put on the windows. Named "*chuang hua*", they are generally much smaller. The paintings put on both sides of a window are called "*chuang pang*" and they are symmetrical as a rule. Above the window, there can also be a painting called "*chuang ding*". All paintings on the window are symbolic patterns of good luck. In North China, people stay on brick beds called "*kang*" which is heated from underneath in winter. The walls along the brick bed are ideal places for New Year paintings, which are called "*san cai*", "*kang wei*" or "*mao fang zi*". In addition, New Year paintings are also found on furniture. "*Zhuo wei*" is hung on the table where people put sacrificial items for gods or family ancestors; "*fu chen zhi*" is put on cupboards where the painting can keep dust from entering the cupboards; "*dou fang*" is a small diamond-shaped painting put on the jars containing rice or water. Finally, there are three more kinds of New Year paintings: "*li hua*", a calendar-like painting put on the kitchen wall or besides the door and painted with seasonal terms in the lunar calendar, so that farmers could check the painting to start sowing or harvest. "*Shen xiang*" are portraits of various gods whom people worship. "*Cao tou hua*" are auspicious paintings put on the doors for oxen, horses, pigs or other domestic animals.

Chinese put New Year paintings of different sizes and subjects at various corners of the house to add more color to the Spring Festival and express good wishes for the coming year. These colorful paintings have deeper cultural meanings. Through these art works, Chinese people aspire for a better life. The paintings reflect the interesting folk culture from religion to details of daily life, which are portrayed in abundant detail in varying genres.

New Year paintings of deities mainly reflect the Chinese people's beliefs. Among the door guardians, there are martial and civil gods. Martial gods include Shen Tu and Yu Lei, Yuchi Gong and Qin Qiong, as well as Zhong Kui. Civil gods mainly include different kinds of Gods of Fortune and other celestial deities in Taoist or Buddhist beliefs. There are also portraits of the Jade Emperor - the supreme deity in Taoism; the three elderly figures representing good luck, high official ranking and longevity; as well as the God of Stove and his wife. New Year paintings of auspicious and festive content embody folk values. They usually rely on homophones to express good wishes. For example, peony flowers in a vase read as "*fu gui ping an*" (rich, prominent and safe), pomegranate and peach mean "*duo fu duo shou*" (good luck and longevity), lotus flowers and carp would translate as "*lian nian you yu*" (surpluses for consecutive years). Such paintings carry through a robust and happy atmosphere. New Year paintings of ancient folk operas reflect folk literature and flourished much later than other types of paintings. People living in the countryside or mountains didn't have many chances to watch folk operas, so they bought such paintings as an entertainment. At that time, such paintings also helped spread culture among different regions. New Year paintings of folk life generally portray farming scenes such as good harvest. In addition, at the end of the Qing Dynasty in the early 20th century, many New Year paintings also reflected current affairs and patriotic themes. Such paintings are especially valuable for studying the social life of that time.

In ancient times, New Year paintings were very popular among the common people thanks to their auspicious meanings, festive atmosphere, low price and portability. In today's China, New Year paintings have once again gained popularity due to their unique cultural values.

New Year paintings feature exaggerated characters with bright and contrasting colors. The ornamental paintings usually carry strong rural and regional characteristics. This book presents some typical New Year paintings from across the country, so that readers can have a rough idea about the distinctive paintings genres in different regions.

#【CONTENTS】

Yangliuqing of Tianjin 1

Taohuawu of Jiangsu 21

Mianzhu of Sichuan 41

Yangjiabu of Shandong 61

Other areas 79

References 102

Yangliuqing of Tianjin

Yangliuqing lies at 15 kilometers to the west of downtown Tianjin. With convenient transportation both on land and water, it has since ancient times been a prosperous commerce center. Originally named Liukou Town, it gained the name "Yangliuqing", meaning "green willows and poplars" in the Ming Dynasty (1368-1644). The farmers in Yangliuqing are also good at painting. Gradually, Yangliuqing New Year painting became one of the country's most famous folk arts.

It was about the end of the Ming Dynasty when local people in Yangliuqing gathered to work on New Year paintings in studios. The painting business peaked during the rule of emperors Qianlong and Jiaqing (1736-1820) of the Qing Dynasty (1644-1911). But it declined by the end of the Qing Dynasty. The business continued in the early 1920s, with as many as 6,000 craftsmen working at the same time. Among the most famous studios were Dailianzeng, Qijianlong, Meili, Jianzengli, Aizhuzhai and Gaoqingyun Old Painting Store.

Yangliuqing New Year paintings cover a wide range of topics with diversified forms. Major subjects include deities' portraits, literary stories, folk customs, current affairs, beauties and children, flowers and birds, fish and insects. Among these subjects, paintings on people carry the strongest regional feature. Generally, the figures portrayed by Yangliuqing artists are tall, stout and their dresses are painted in details. Different lines are applied to bring out characters whose faces and gestures are dramatically different. Most figures have white faces with pink cheeks. The lines of the face are lightly colored. In the early years, Yangliuqing New Year paintings focused on people and the lines were casual. But gradually, the design became more complicated with elegant background. For different paintings, Yangliuqing artists used woodblock printing, dyeing or filling pigments in frames. Most of the colors used in Yangliuqing are soft and subdued (local artists call them "soft colors"), while bright colors ("hard colors") are rarely used. In general, Yangliuqing New Year paintings are elegant, simple and unaffected, with thin and clear lines that are well designed.

Door guardians, early Qing Dynasty (1644-1911)

Ancient Chinese New Year paintings were mostly made in pairs. This was especially the case with door guardian paintings. This set portrays two guardians in full armor. The guardian on the left has round eyes, thick eye browses and tough curling bristles; the other has narrow eyes, thin eye browses and long beard. They are most probably Tang Dynasty (AD 618-907) generals Yuchi Gong and Qin Qiong who were idolized as door guardians in the Yuan and Ming dynasties (1271-1644). The generals are portrayed with vivid expressions and detailed clothing. Different kinds of lines are applied on the two figures' faces to bring out their contrasting characteristics. The simple and unaffected coloring is typical of the early works in Yangliuqing.

Door guardians, Qing Dynasty

This pair of door guardian paintings are also about Tang Dynasty generals Qin Qiong (right) and Yuchi Gong, who aided Li Shimin to found the Tang Dynasty more than 1,400 years ago. Storytellers and popular novels in the Yuan and Ming dynasties added imaginative details to the lives of the two devoted generals, who eventually became the most important door guardians in the country. Qin Qiong has a pale skin with narrow eyes and long beard, using the golden mace in battles; Yuchi Gong, on the other hand, has crimson face with round eyes and curling bristles, using the iron nodular staff. Compared with the previous pair of paintings, this set is much more elaborately done. The background features clouds and the auspicious utensils used by the Eight Immortals in folklore. The colors on the face and hands of the figures are applied manually, while all other parts of the paintings are block-printed. Such kind of paintings with refined figures and complicated background were made in the later years of Yangliuqing.

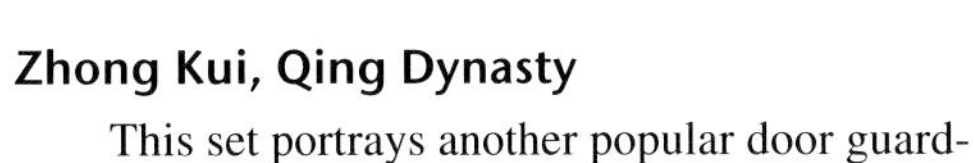

Zhong Kui, Qing Dynasty

This set portrays another popular door guardian known as Zhong Kui. Legends say Zhong Kui was a man with martial arts who didn't pass the imperial exams to become an official. He died in front of the imperial palace and became ruler of the ghosts. It is said that he once caught and swallowed the evil ghosts that disturbed Emperor Xuanzong of the Tang Dynasty (AD 618-907). Thus the emperor ordered painters to make a portrait of Zhong Kui, which was a way to honor the deceased. Later on, the common folks regarded Zhong Kui as a door guardian and believed he could fend off evil spirits. Zhong Kui is usually portrayed as ugly and vicious-looking. Wearing a hat, he holds a sword in hand. He is always dressed in blue robe and wears leather boots. A red bat follows him. In this set of New Year paintings, Zhong Kui wears elegant official robe which is a different version developed among the folks. The paintings also carry the seal of Qijianlong New Year Painting Studio.

Five children contending for championship, Qing Dynasty

In the picture, five children vie for the lotus. This inage implies that the five children contend for championship, they would pass the imperial examinations, and the children themselves are auspicious symbols of prosperity. It is one of the most favored pictures by the ordinary people.

Auspiciousness, late Qing Dynasty

The picture is usually pasted at the lanterns on the screen wall. The background of the picture is the Chinese character "*fu*" (good fortune) and the auspicious symbol in Buddhism. The child has various mascots in his hands. It is one of the New Year pictures favored by folks.

Successive harvest, Qing Dynasty

The picture is titled *Successive harvest* (*lian nian you yu*) which is similar to lotus and fish in pronunciation. The images of plump baby, gold fish and lotus are not only pleasant to the eyes, but also imply more wealth and sons, which is very popular among the folks.

Triple fortune and longevity, Qing Dynasty

Fingered citron (right), peach (middle) and pomegranate are placed together to imply the triple meanings: more fortune (fingered citron), more longevity (peach) and more children (pomegranate). Three young boys hold the auspicious fruits. It is a common image in the baby New Year paintings of Yangliuqing.

Wintry entertainment, late Qing Dynasty

This painting portrays frolicking children. It also serves as a clever game to count the winter days. The painting has three folk opera excerpts' names written in hollowed out strokes. By filling in one stroke everyday, one could count all the 81 wintry days on the traditional Chinese lunar calendar. When all stokes were filled, spring would arrive. The seven little children are staging the three operas. The painting is rendered with soft colors, intricate lines, and decorated with mountains and rivers, trees and rocks.

Stealing the immortal grass, Qing Dynasty

This painting depicts a scene from *The Tale of the White Snake*, which is about the tragic love between a scholar and a young lady who was actually a white snake. This painting is set in the scene when the scholar named Xu Xian fell ill, Lady White Snake (right) and her younger sister Lady Green Snake (middle) tried to steal an immortal grass to save him. They met the Crane Boy (left) who was guarding the grass and they staged a fierce battle. This painting has elegant coloring and a well-balanced structure with simple rocks as the background. It is a typical work of Yangliuqing.

Ladies with babies, mid-Qing Dynasty

This pair of paintings belongs to the genre of beauties and babies, which symbolizes harmonious family life. The ladies in the paintings wear typical Qing Dynasty dresses that make them elegant and genteel. The babies wear embroidered bibs and a piece of cloth to cover the belly. They each hold the lotus (*lian* in Chinese), the musical instrument called *sheng*, sweet-scented osmanthus (*gui*) and pomegranate (which has many seeds - *zi*). Together the four items read as *lian sheng gui zi* - bearing a number of sons who would become high-ranking officials, which was a dream for Chinese women in the feudal society. The painting was hand-dyed and represents the mature period of Yangliuqing works.

Guan Yu and the Gods of Fortune, Qing Dynasty

This painting depicts two Gods of Fortune and Guan Yu, an important character in *Romance of the Three Kingdoms.* Guan Yu (with crimson face) had many virtues and in succeeding dynasties he was portrayed as an ideal man with both strength and intelligence. As he gives priority to righteousness and despises fortune, folk legends often put him above the status of the God of Fortune. In this painting, the two Gods of Fortune sit below Guan Yu. One of them wears a red robe and holds a shoe-shaped gold ingot used as money; the other wears green robe and holds an S-shaped ornament named *ruyi* - or fulfiling one's wishes. Below them is a treasure bowl. The three main characters all have an escort. The top of the painting is decorated with the pattern of two dragons playing with a jewel. The whole work is adorned richly.

Leaping over the Tanxi River, Qing Dynasty

This painting depicts the story of Liu Bei being chased by Cai Mao in the classic novel *Romance of the Three Kingdoms.* Liu Bei, who would found the Kingdom of Shu, is leaping over the Tanxi River on his horse. Cai Mao, a general who serves Cao Cao, founder of the Kingdom of Wei, does not dare to leap into the surging waves. The Chinese characters on top of the painting refer to the title of the excerpt from the folk opera. The painting has strong strokes and dark colors. The waves are painted in the traditional techniques.

Pavilion of the Three Worlds, Qing Dynasty

Inside the hexagon pavilion is the tablet of the deities in charge of the heaven, the earth and the nether world. Triangular flags are put on the top of the pavilion, flowery patters adorn the roof, with jade musical instrument, red bat, gold coin and jewelry dangling at the corners. The tablet is enshrined on lotus base. The pavilion also has banisters. The well-designed work has golden block print, which indicates its expensive price.

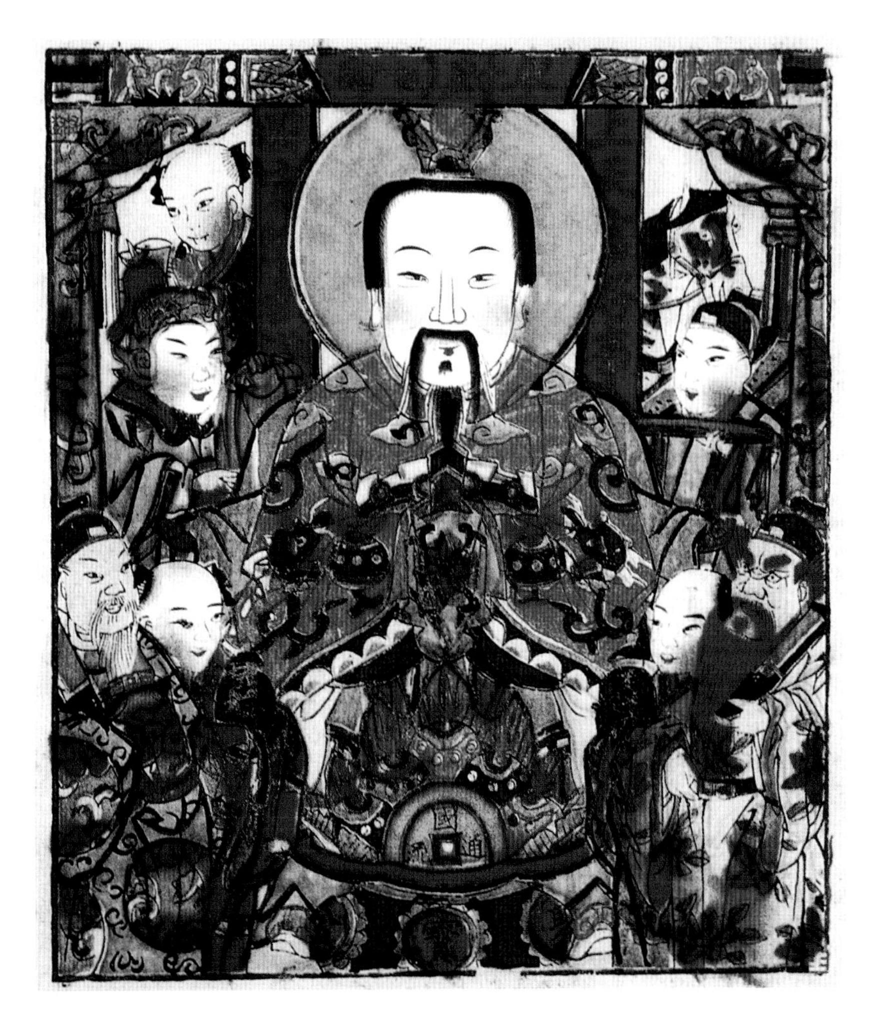

God of Stove, Qing Dynasty

The God of Stove in this painting wears a red robe with boa design and a green aura. The common folks nicknamed such kind of painting as "Big Green Head", which was worshiped by the families of princes and high-ranking officials in the Qing Dynasty. The God of Stove stands behind a treasure bowl, with an assistant, an accountant and two boys standing beside him. Niches used for worshiping are painted around them. The colors were applied by woodblock printing, only the characters' faces were dyed. Such kind of paintings has many figures and interesting contents that bring out a strong effect.

Peaceful four seasons, Qing Dynasty

The set depicts vases with flowers. The two vases are painted on one piece of paper, one needs to cut them into two before putting them on the wall. The peony, lotus, chrysanthemum and plum flowers symbolize spring, summer, autumn and winter. In Chinese, vase is pronounced as *ping*, the same as peaceful. Thus the painting means peaceful four seasons. Pomegranate, fingered citron and peach beside the vases represent good fortunes and longevity. The painting is elegant and refined, typical of the works of Yangliuqing.

Taohuawu of Jiangsu

Taohuawu is located in Suzhou of East China's Jiangsu Province. Since the Song Dynasty (960-1279), Taohuawu has been a cultural center with flourishing handicrafts business. Craftsmen in Taohuawu began making New Year paintings in the Ming Dynasty (1368-1644) and the place soon became a center of New Year paintings in southern China. Unfortunately, most of the early paintings were destroyed in the warfare before the Qing Dynasty (1644-1911) was established. Only a few precious works are preserved in Japan. Nowadays, the ancient Taohuawu New Year paintings treasured in China date back to the rule of Emperor Guangxu (1871-1908) of the Qing Dynasty. Paintings made in the mid-Qing Dynasty are rarely found.

Taohuawu's New Year painting industry reached its peak at the turn of the Ming and Qing dynasties in the 17th century. The more than 40 workshops were exporting paintings to Japan and Southeast Asia, which also influenced the painting style of these regions. From the few well-preserved paintings, historians have identified painting studios named Zhangxingju, Weihongtai and Luyunlin, which were the early studios; whereas Wangrongxing and Hongyunge appeared much later.

In its long history, New Year paintings in Taohuawu covered almost all the subjects and forms of this unique folk painting genre. Besides being hand-painted, there were also block-printed works. The colors were applied directly, with water, or by woodblock printing. In general, New Year paintings in Taohuawu are light and elegant. The lean characters are drawn with thin and close lines. Peach pink is a striking color of the paintings from Taohuawu, which literally means Peach Flower Village Port. The baby paintings at Taohuawu are especially interesting. In addition to the common baby playing subject, craftsmen at Taohuawu also created a unique "*Tuan A Fu*" style that features a chubby baby in the shape of a perfect circle. Because such a figure symbolizes fulfillment, harmony and good fortunes, this kind of baby painting attracted many customers and influenced other New Year painting centers such as Tantou of nearby Hunan Province.

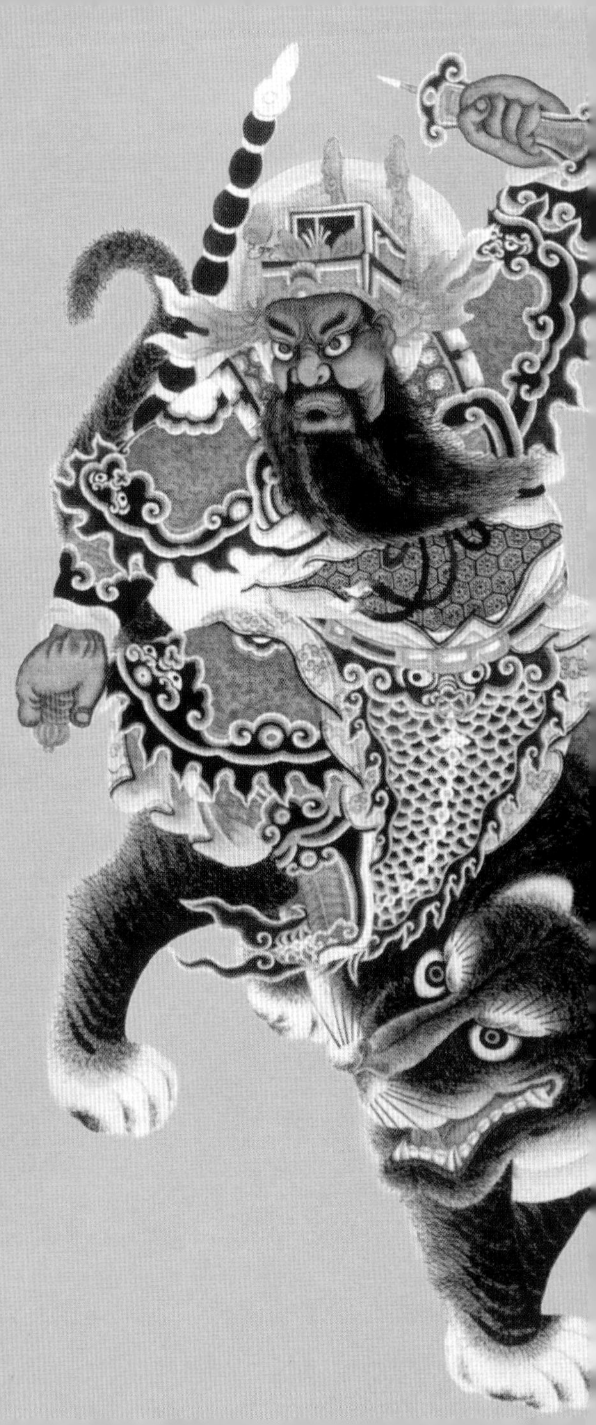

王荣兴出品

Five babies and the door guardians, Qing Dynasty

The main figures in the set are the door guardians Qin Qiong and Yuchi Gong who are fully armored, holding axe, golden mace and iron nodular staff. In front of them are five babies, who come from the household tale of five children who grew up to become high-ranking officials. The child at the center rides on the kylin - an imaginary auspicious animal which legends say is responsible for sending a newborn baby to a family. The paintings feature tight lines with block-printed colors, except for the face where the color is hand-painted. The characters are styled similar to those in Yangjiabu of Shandong Province, but the face paint is closer to the style of Miaozhu works in Sichuan Province. This reflects the exchanges of artistic elements in different regions.

Zhong Kui, Qing Dynasty

This set is also about the door guardian. The figure wears a hat of the judge and holds a tablet symbolizing official ranking in hand. The hat and the little ghost that follows the judge prove that this is Zhong Kui, a popular door guardian who is in charge of all ghosts. A spider dangles in front of Zhong Kui. In southern China, people believe that spiders could bring good luck and call them "happy spiders". Ancient craftsmen printed the figures first, then applied color with block printing. The hair and moustache of the figures are depicted in detail; the coloring of the whole work is striking, both of which are representative of Taohuawu New Year paintings.

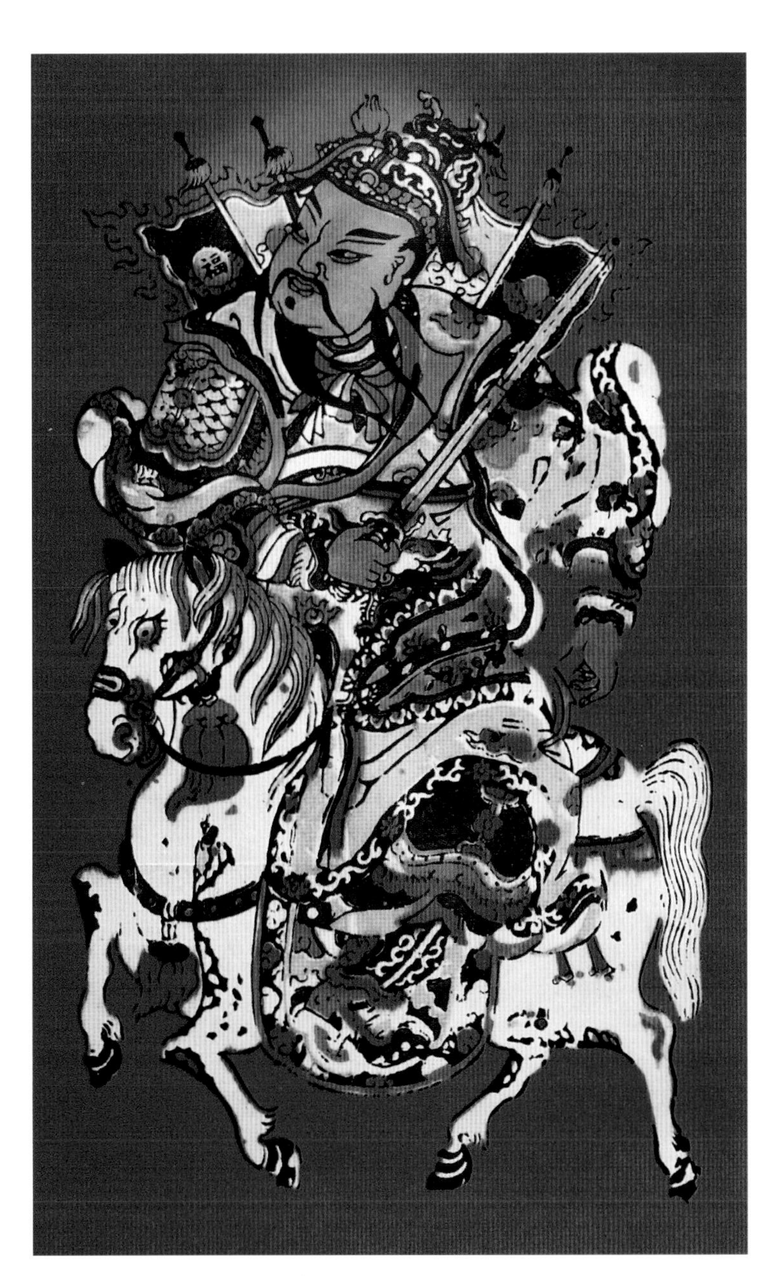

Mace and staff on the horse, Qing Dynasty

The figures in this set of paintings hold the golden mace and iron nodular staff, which indicate that they are the popular door guardians Qin Qiong (right) and Yuchi Gong. The two generals ride on white and red horses. Fully armed, they both look serious. The armor they wear is obviously influenced by the Peking Opera costumes of the time. The two galloping horses are well designed with glaring eyes. The lines in the set are thin and tightly drawn. The soft color is set against a crimson background which is rare among the New Year paintings in Taohuawu.

Harmony and auspiciousness, Qing Dynasty

This is a typical "*Tuan A Fu*" painting which is unique for Taohuawu. The chubby babies wear brocade clothes and hold a scroll written with "*he qi zhi xiang*" - harmony and auspiciousness. Above the babies are bats carrying the fingered citron and peach which are written with "*ruyi*" - be perfectly satisfied. With red as the reigning color, the painting also has some green, purple and yellow, which make the work very joyful. Such kind of baby painting is only found in Taohuawu and it has gained great popularity.

Pipa player, late Qing Dynasty

This painting depicts people of the lower stretches of the Yangtze River watching a *tanci* storytelling performance. The storyteller at the right side of the painting plays *pipa*, a pluck-stringed instrument, while telling a story in the musical local dialect. Facing her is a lady holding a puppy and she is immersed in the story. Another lady, however, turns around to look at her children playing nearby. The poem at the upper right corner sings praise of the storyteller's great talents and how she tells a story full of emotion. The ladies in the painting are gentle and elegant, which is typical of the lady paintings in Taohuawu.

Ten beauties playing the ball, late Qing Dynasty

The painting features ten women of Han nationality and Manchurian ethnic minority. The subject bears strong influence from the democracy thoughts in the late Qing Dynasty which advocated the idea that Han and Manchurian belonged to the same family and that men and women were equal. In early Qing Dynasty, there were social differences between the Han people and the Manchurian rulers who came from Northeast China to unify the whole country. The painting is not very refined, but the women wear different kinds of dresses that make it rather valuable. The ten women play the ball on a bridge. In the background are buildings along the river, which is a perfect scene of the people's lives in eastern China where there are many rivers and lakes.

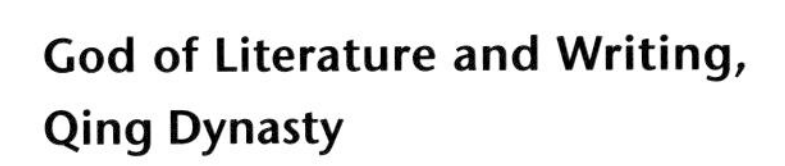

God of Literature and Writing, Qing Dynasty

Kuixing, or the God of Literature and Writing, was the most important deity for ancient scholars. Because the word "*kui*", or the champion in the imperial examination, is formed with "*gui*" (ghost) and "*dou*" (the Big Dipper), ancient painters depicted the God of Literature and Writing as a ghost kicking at the Big Dipper. Traditionally, the four stars in the bowl of the Big Dipper are called Kuixing, or the stars for the God of Literature and Writer. Wearing animal skin and colorful ribbon, the ghost stands with one foot on a dragon, with a brush in one hand and a gold ingot in another, which means that the God of Literature and Writer also sends good fortunes to people. The painting does a good job with the ghost, the dragon's scales and expression are also attractive.

Monkey King plays havoc in heaven, Qing Dynasty

This painting depicts a scene from the popular classic novel *Journey to the West.* When Monkey King finds out that the Jade Emperor only appointed him to be a petty official in charge of the horses in heaven, he is outrageous and plays havoc in heaven. At the top right corner, the heavenly troop are chasing after the Monkey King, who holds his golden stick at the left corner. Above the Monkey King, the Taoist deity Taishang Laojun and the Buddhist Goddess of Mercy (Guanshiyin) both try to conquer the Monkey King with different tools. The figures in the painting are well designed and the clouds are vividly depicted. Red, yellow and purple are the main harmonious colors.

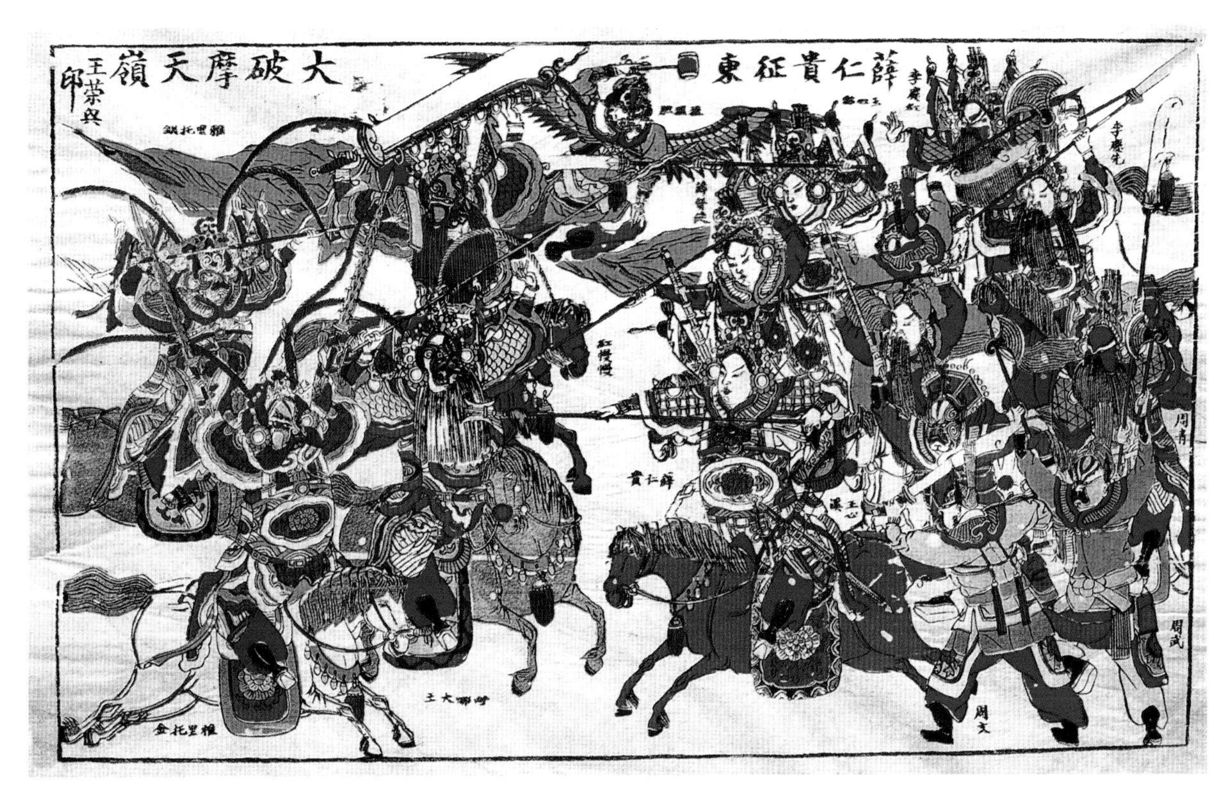

Battle at Motianlin, Qing Dynasty

This painting is about Tang Dynasty (AD 618-907) general Xue Rengui conquering enemies at Motianlin. The general riding on the red horse is Xue Rengui. To his left are his adversaries Xinxindan and Hongmanman. This is a grand painting with multiple characters whose costumes were inspired by those from Peking Opera. Each character is named and the seal of Wang Rongxing is inscribed at the top left corner.

Eight Immortals celebrate God of Longevity's birthday, Qing Dynasty

This painting depicts the legendary Eight Immortals who are celebrating the birthday of the God of Longevity. A monkey offers a big peach to the God of Longevity, who is surrounded by Lu Dongbin, the Goddess of Lotus and six other immortals who are popular in folk legends. The two deities of harmony and peace are painted on both sides of the painting with dragon and phoenix. The figures are not painted with great care, but the composition and coloring of the painting make it an excellent work of art.

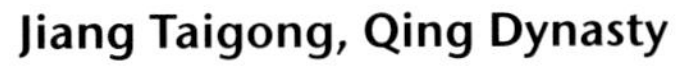

Jiang Taigong, Qing Dynasty

This painting is about Jiang Taigong, or Jiang Ziya, who helped Ji Chang and his son Ji Fa to topple the decadent Shang Dynasty and found the Zhou Dynasty in the 11th century BC. Jiang has been praised as an example of virtuous official to aid imperial rulers. In the painting, the smiling Jiang rides on an auspicious animal, with a taichi mirror in one hand and a yellow flag in another. The painting is surrounded by the Chinese character of longevity. The legendary animal steps on *ruyi*, an ornament that symbolizes fulfillment of wishes. Though the painting is not refined, the animal is depicted with complicated and striking lines. Green and yellow are the reigning colors that make the painting peaceful and auspicious.

Character of Longevity, Qing Dynasty

The Chinese character "*shou*" (寿) means long life. This painting features "*shou*" against a blue background. It seems to be a counterpart of another painting featuring the character "*fu*" (*fortune*). Together they mean "Enjoying Fortune and Longevity". In the print of Longevity are usually painted the Gods of Good Fortune, Wealth and Longevity, Eight Immortals Crossing the Sea. The images of deer, crane, pine, pavilions, clouds among others are also in praise of longevity.

Fu - good fortune, Qing Dynasty

The painting is about the Chinese character "*fu*" (福) - good fortune, longevity, affluence, peace and harmony. This is one of the most beloved words for good wishes in China. The word is painted against a yellow background, with the deities of peace and harmony on the character. Another deity is sending good fortune and the kylin is sending a baby to the world. Peony and osmanthus flowers are painted beneath the word "*fu*", both of which symbolize affluence and high official ranking. The painting has multiple figures that are all very well designed and painted.

Small red God of Stove, late Qing Dynasty

This portrait of the God of Stove was worshiped by common families in Suzhou. The small painting was printed on red paper. The God of Stove wears a crown, a golden pendant, heavenly official dress and is seated on a special chair for deities. The ornament above him has lotus flower and golden coin decoration, with golden musical instrument and double fish pendants. A treasure bowel is painted at the bottom. Two immortals representing harmony and peace stand beside the God of Stove. The printed art work has light and dark blue coloring that makes it elegant and extraordinary.

Auspicious flowers and fruits, Qing Dynasty

The vase in the painting has peony flowers, pomegranate and peach which represent prestige, multiple children and longevity. The background has *qin* (music instrument), *go* (Chinese chess), books and paintings which stand for elegant pursuit. The vase is vividly depicted, the flowers are painted with bright colors which match well with the elegant vase. This is a high level work on festival mood from Taohuawu.

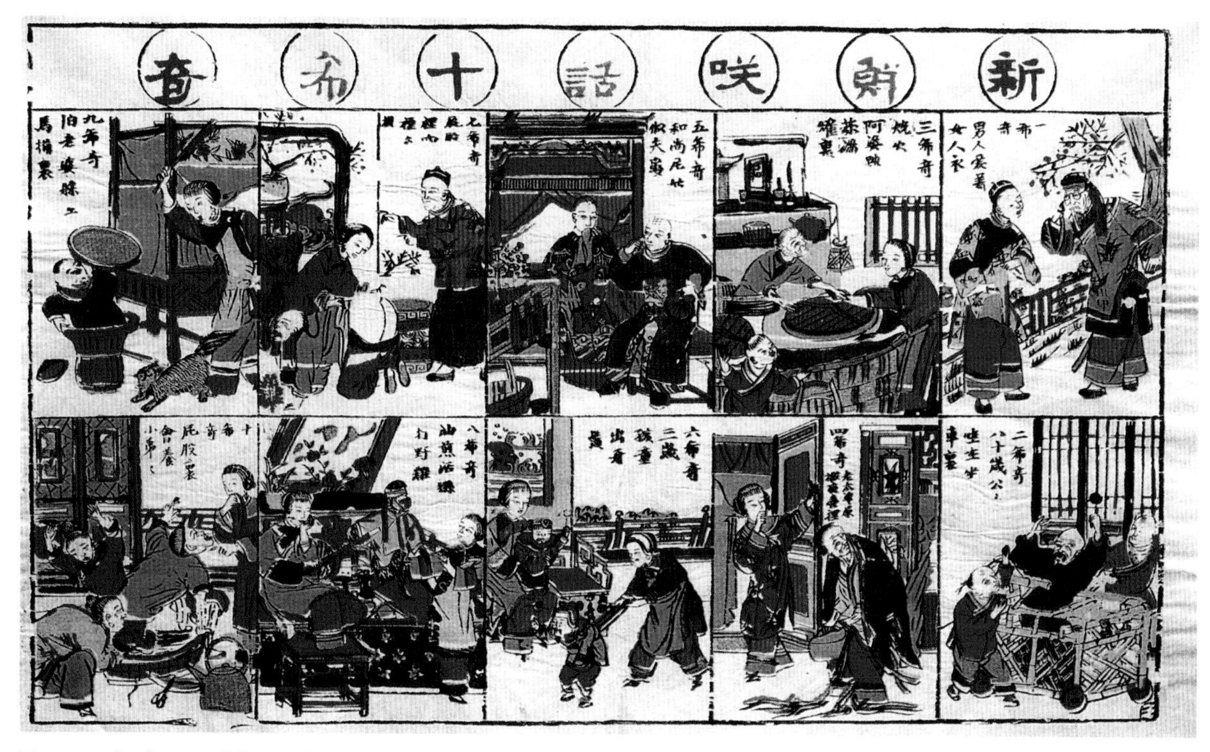

Ten comical new things, Qing Dynasty

This painting depicts some bizarre happenings at the end of the Qing Dynasty. The so-called comical new things, such as “men dressed like women”, “frying a monkey and shooting a pheasant”, reflect the dark side of the society. But the figures are well designed and block printed with pink and purple, which are typical of Taohuawu works. The painting is separated into ten smaller squares like a serial cartoon. Such paintings were popular at the end of the Qing Dynasty. In addition, the interior decoration depicted here is valuable for researchers on Qing Dynasty history.

Mianzhu of Sichuan

Sichuan Province of Southwest China is another production center of New Year paintings. Mianzhu in its northwest, Liangping in its east, and Jiajiang in its south are known for their art works. New Year paintings from Mianzhu are the most famous and influential. They are sold to neighboring provinces of Shaanxi, Qinghai, Hunan and Hubei, even abroad to Japan and Southeast Asia.

According to Song Dynasty (960-1279) books titled *Records of Chengdu's Past and Present* (*Chengdu Gujin Ji*) by Zhao Dang and *Records of the Flourishing Dream in the Eastern Capital* (*Dongjing Menghua Lu*) by Meng Yuanlao, a New Year painting market had appeared in Chengdu in the Song Dynasty. This probably means that Mianzhu also started making this folk painting at that time. By the rules of emperors Qianlong and Jiangqing of the mid-Qing Dynasty (1644-1911), Mianzhu New Year painting business had reached its peak, with more than 300 studios.

The New Year paintings in Mianzhu cover a wide variety of subjects. Similar to other New Year painting production centers, Mianzhu craftsmen also began with door guardians and gradually developed themes on festival and folk operas. Because Mianzhu is locked in deep mountains, transportation has been rather poor until recent decades. However, this has contributed to the formation of a unique style of New Year paintings. Comparatively, door guardian paintings reached a higher artistic level than folk opera paintings. Though the door guardian paintings feature simple designs and don't use colorful block printing, the simple images painted by hand are quite powerful and attractive.

Mianzhu New Year paintings can be roughly categorized as "red products" and "black products". The former is mainly about door guardians, young ladies, children and folk legends. Lines of the figures are drawn first before the colors are applied by hand. The "black products" include portraits of deities, stories and scenes of farmers working in the fields and their wives weaving at home. Such paintings are printed with wood blocks and black ink. There is another kind of painting nicknamed "*tianshuizu*", which means the paintings are done in a hurry with leftover pigments. They are sold to poor families. Although the lines are not refined, such paintings are rustic and have a different flavor than most New Year paintings.

Door guardians, Qing Dynasty

The door guardians in this set of paintings wear full armor and hold a broad sword in hand. One guardian looks boorish, while the other seems more self-composed. But both are serious and mighty. It is hard to guess the identity of these guardians. But the paintings are really well done, with the armor and weapon painted in great details. The whirling cloud pattern on the armor and the guardians' faces are dyed carefully to be harmonious. The paintings involve techniques from the Song Dynasty (960-1279), which makes them very precious.

Door guardians, Qing Dynasty

The golden mace and iron nodular staff held by the guardians indicate that they are Tang Dynasty (AD 618-907) generals Qin Qiong and Yuchi Gong. Qin Qiong has a pale skin with narrow eyes and long beard, he uses the golden mace in battles; Yuchi Gong, on the other hand, has crimson face with round eyes and curling bristles, he uses the iron nodular staff. The figures are simple, featuring red and green as the main colors. The face and hands are pink. The coloring is bright and the overall style is simple but powerful. It represents the typical style of Mianzhu New Year paintings.

Qin Qiong and Yuchi Gong, Qing Dynasty

This set again is about the popular door guardians Qin Qiong and Yuchi Gong. The two generals are of contrasting characters - Yuchi Gong (left) is boorish and Qin Qiong is scholarly. Their clothes are given full details, part of the clothes seems to be flying in the wind. Standing like bows, the two generals are portrayed with a natural air. Their faces don't have any pigments, while their armor is decorated with small golden flowers. This is an excellent example of Mianzhu works.

Golden mace and iron nodular staff, Qing Dynasty

This pair of paintings is also about Qin Qiong and Yuchi Gong. The two door guardians wear hats and robes while displaying their golden mace and iron nodular staff. The outline is woodblock printed, with vivid expression and simple designing. But the clothing is rather sketchy, which shows this is a "*tianshuizu*" type of painting done in a hurry and sold at a low price.

Gods of Fortune, Qing Dynasty

The Gods of Fortune uphold an incense burner, which means that the customer who buys this painting has paid tribute to the heavenly deities in the hope of gaining higher official ranking. The figures are done in a simple but powerful way. The Gods of Fortune have wrinkles on the forehead, showing old age. The cloud pattern on their shoes and the sleeves are elegant. The coloring is bright and simple. The hand-applied rouge on the face and hands is a unique feature of Mianzhu New Year paintings. On the robe, small flowers are printed with gold, which adds an interesting detail to the painting.

Children holding the vase, late Qing Dynasty

The image of children holding vases with peony flowers symbolizes affluence and peace. Such kind of paintings is generally put on the door of the bedroom. The children in the paintings are designed simply, but the expression is rather dull. The coat is dyed green and red, the trousers blue and green, marked with black lines. Although this is not the best of Mianzhu works, it represents the region's straight-forward style.

Civil and martial Gods of Fortune, Qing Dynasty

The painting presents the civil and martial Gods of Fortune, with the former wearing a red robe and holding an ivory tablet used by high-ranking officials; while the latter wearing green robe above golden armor and holding an iron nodular staff. Between them are a treasure bowl and a treasure tree. The deities have a calm and peaceful expression, with an aura behind them. The tree's trunk and branches are painted in detail. But the coloring is rather casual and fails to add more value to the painting.

Double Flag Gate, Qing Dynasty

This is a painting on a folk opera story. Titled *Shuang Qi Men* (*Double Flag Gate*), the story dates back to the turn of the Shang and Zhou dynasties in the 11th century BC. Princess Longji wanted her husband Hongjin to help Jiang Ziya in the fight against the cruel King Zhou of Shang Dynasty. But Hongjin's father didn't want him to become a rebel. Hongjin had to engage in a battle against the troops of Zhou, which was led by Jiang Ziya. Princess Longji deployed her troops according to the Outer Flag Gate Strategy, which conquered her husband's Inner Flag Gate Strategy. Finally, the couple persuaded their father to surrender to Jiang Ziya. The couple in the painting is lanky, rigid and exaggerated. Wearing Peking Opera masks, they all don operatic costumes. Where the color is light, one can see complex lines for the costumes. Green, blue, red and yellow are the main colors that make the painting bright and eye-catching.

Interlocking stratagems, Qing Dynasty

This story comes from the classic novel *Romance of the Three Kingdoms.* At the end of the Eastern Han Dynasty in the 3rd century, Dong Zhuo controlled the imperial court and nobody could overthrow the corrupt minister because a mighty general named Lu Bu had become his adopted son. Patriotic official Wang Yun thought of a plan with his maid Diao Chan, who later became one of four top beauties in ancient Chinese history. Wang Yun showed Diao Chan to both Dong Zhuo and Lu Bu, and made them become enemies until the young man killed Dong Zhuo. The painting shows how Lu Bu was enchanted by the beauty after a banquet. The old man behind them is Wang Yun, who is quite happy that his plan has worked. Though the figures are not best colored, this is a dramatic scene well presented.

Bodhidharma crossing the river, Qing Dynasty

This painting is about a famous religious figure - Bodhidharma, who came to China in the 6th century to spread Buddhism and became the founder of Chan Sect in the country. In the painting, Bodhidharma holds a staff on which are his grass shoes. In bare feet, the Buddhist master walks across the river on reeds. The figure riding on a dragon behind him is an arhat, an enlightened being in Buddhist beliefs. The painting excels in the powerful lines of waves and clouds. The two main figures are vivid and colored brightly, though a little bit casually.

Treasure tree, Qing Dynasty

The painting is about a folk story on a poor farmer named Cui Wenrui who had the good luck of gaining the heart of a fairy named Zhang Sijie. The fairy planted a treasure tree and the family became rich overnight. In the painting, the couple is looking at children picking coins. This painting is in the same style with the previous two works. They might be dated to the same period from the same studio. Although only of average level, this paining of treasure tree is quite popular and representative in Sichuan Province.

Sanduo Hall, Qing Dynasty

The Village God and Goddess stand at the Sanduo Hall. A treasure bowl is put on a long table inside the hall. The smiling Village God and Goddess hold the golden ingot, with an aura behind them. It's not clear who are the two persons below the eaves. The hall has a horizontal board on the hall written with "*San Duo Tang*" - Hall of Multiple Fortune, Longevity, Multiple Offspring. The people are simply designed and brightly colored. But the interior of the hall is painted in great detail, which is rare in Mianzhu.

Gambling of the rich, early Republic of China(1912-1949)

The picture implies the remonstrance against gambling and avarice. Animals are personified as a satire of the rich.

Yangjiabu of Shandong

One can find many New Year painting production centers in East China's Shandong Province, such as Weixian, Qufu, Gaomi and Pingdu. Since the Ming Dynasty (1368-1644), these areas have been supplying farmers in northern China with New Year paintings. The paintings made in Weixian County of eastern Shandong are also known as Yangjiabu New Year paintings. Together with works of Yangliuqing in Tianjin, Taohuawu in Jiangsu and Mianzhu of Sichuan, they are known as the four most famous New Year painting genres in China. Until today, Yangjiabu is still an important production center of New Year paintings, and the Yangjiabu New Year painting has been listed as one of the first intangible cultural relics in China.

According to the Yang Family pedigree, the family's ancestors moved to Weifang of Shandong from Sichuan in the Ming Dynasty in the late 14th century. They started making New Year paintings and focused on portraits of various deities. By the Qing Dynasty in the mid-17th century, local craftsmen had absorbed other cultural elements and included more content in their paintings, such as driving away evils, celebrating festivals and local folk opera excerpts. With their distinctive style, Yangjiabu New Year painting studios numbered more than 100 at its peak and opened many branches in other provinces. The most famous studios were Gongmao, Yongsheng and Wanshun.

Because Yangjiabu craftsmen made portraits of deities in the early days, their works were influenced by religious woodblock prints and featured strict designing. Later, they were influenced by illustrations in Ming Dynasty novels and the lines became smooth and flowing. In the Qing Dynasty, learning from works of Yangliuqing and Taohuawu, Yangjiabu craftsmen finally established their own style that relied heavily on colorful woodblock printing and used contrasting colors such as red vs. green and yellow vs. purple, but giving them equally small space. The people depicted in Yangjiabu paintings are not as muscular as those in Yangliuqing, nor as gentle as those in Taohuawu. But compared with Yangliuqing, Yangjiabu New Year paintings tend to portray people as having the same face, the only distinctions are their hairstyle and dresses.

Light-Holding Master and Zhao Gongming, Qing Dynasty

The set of paintings feature two characters from the ancient novel *Creation of the Gods* (*Feng Shen Yanyi*). Zhao Gongming and the Light-Holding Master were engaged in the battles at the end of the Shang Dynasty. Zhao, who was helping the Shang ruler, rides on an auspicious animal, holding a golden ingot and a sword; the Light-Holding Master, who aids Jiang Ziya, rides on a sika deer, holding a *ruyi* - an s-shaped jade ornament and another religious instrument. In front of them are their symbolic tools: Zhao Gongming uses a pair of golden scissors that can change into dragons; the Light-Holding Master uses the Buddhist beads. Although the two characters look alike, their age difference is well represented through lines and colors. There are some minor defects in the woodblock printed coloring, but it's already quite an interesting work. The anonymous painter applied bold red on the characters' faces. The bright colors on the armor and the animals they ride are surprisingly harmonious.

月

Children with heavenly officials, Qing Dynasty

This is about the civil door guardian - the heavenly official who blesses the world. Wearing an official hat, embroidered robe and holding an ivory tablet, the heavenly official greets everyone with a broad grin. He is surrounded by five young boys, who hold the incense burner, vase, peony and lotus flowers, as well as colorful lantern - symbols of good luck, high official ranking, fulfilling all the good wishes and affluence. Above the figures are patterns of the phoenix and peony flowers. Inside the flowers are written with the words "sun" and "moon". The characters are painted close to each other but well featured. The lines are smooth and flowing; the coloring is bright and harmonious. This is a representative work at the peak of Yangjiabu New Year painting production.

Liu Hai teases the golden toad, Qing Dynasty

Liu Hai is a popular figure in folk legends. It is said he pursued Taoist practices and lived as a hermit in Huashan of Shaanxi before becoming an immortal. Legends say that he is one of the deities sending good fortune to the world. In this painting, Liu Hai holds some copper coins to tease a golden toad at his foot. This is a typical image when folk artists potray Liu Hai. With round face, Liu Hai is depicted with simple lines. His clothes and the toad are colored brightly, which is a typical style of Yangjiabu works. Before putting on the painting, one needs to cut it into two and put it on both doors.

Children and lions entering the door, Qing Dynasty

Two children ride on the lions while playing the colorful ball. There are two smaller lions in the painting and the title of the painting "*shi tong jin men*" is written on the side. But there are different explanations to the name. Some experts believe this indicates that the children are paying tribute to their teacher (*shi* could mean both "teacher" and "lion") at the beginning of their studies; others say this painting expresses the wish that the children could grow as strong as the lion; still some believe it means that people hope more sons were born to the family. The characters in the painting are of average level, but the coloring is rather harmonious.

Announcing good news, sending official title, Qing Dynasty

This painting is also on the theme of young children. One of the two children holds a branch with orange, pomegranate and apricot. In Chinese legends, the three fruits are called "*sanyuan*" - three round fruits, but it also sounds the same as the top three winners in the imperial exam. The other child drags a small cart carrying official hat and golden ingot. A colorful phoenix stands on the child's hand, announcing the good news that a member of the family has excelled in the imperial exam to become an official. The children are depicted slightly out of balance, but the clothes and other instruments are vivid. Such a subject is very popular in Shandong.

Auspicious spring, early Republic of China (1912-1949)

This painting depicts a cock singing towards the rising sun on a rock. In Chinese, cock (*ji*) sounds similar with auspiciousness. The peony flowers and red sun also stand for good luck and affluence in folklore. The painting is designed in a circle, which is termed "moonlight" among folk artists. Such festive themes are often used as window decorations.

Celebrating the Lantern Festival, Qing Dynasty

Ten young children are celebrating the Lantern Festival, which falls on the 15th day of the first lunar month. It is traditionally seen as the end of the long Spring Festival celebrations. The children play with various lanterns and toys. Golden ingots and copper coins are scattered on the ground to add more festive atmosphere. The child in the center holds a lantern shaped like the legendary turtle's head, which expresses the hope that the child would grow up to succeed as number one in the imperial exam. The interior scene offers a glimpse to the traditional home decoration. Also printed with woodblock, the painting features big patches of yellow, which is seldom seen in paintings from Yangjiabu.

God of Fortune comes home, Qing Dynasty

In northern China, people believe that the God of Fortune comes back to the family after visiting the heaven on the fifth day of the first lunar month. This painting shows the God of Fortune leading the Boys of Fortune and heavenly official in charge of business to send good fortune to the family. The God of Fortune is portrayed as a rural landlord knocking on the door. To his left, the two Boys of Fortune hold a big golden ingot; to his right, the heavenly official pushes a cart of treasure. The characters are simple, but the colors are bright. The architecture of the time is well depicted.

Big fortune comes rolling in, Qing Dynasty

This is about the martial door guardian Zhao Gongming sending good fortune upon the lunar New Year. Zhao Gongming rides on a cloud and the tiger with him pours out numerous golden ingots onto the ground. The landlord and children carry the ingots back home. A lady stands by the door, looking immensely pleased. The title "*da fa cai yuan*" (big fortune comes rolling in) is written above the painting. With simple structure and elegant coloring, the painting features lanky figures which is rarely seen in Yangjiabu works. The building to the left is very well painted.

Jinshan Temple, Qing Dynasty

This painting depicts a scene from the popular folk legend *Tale of the White Snake*. After a young scholar named Xu Xian got married with a lady who was actually a white snake, a monk named Fahai abducted Xu Xian to the Jinshan Temple and tried to force him to leave his wife and child. Lady White Snake and her younger sister Lady Green Snake attempted to save Xu Xian by inundating the temple. In the painting, Lady White Snake stands on the boat, her sister sits behind her, a sea monster and a marine deity have emerged to help them. Facing them, Xu Xian sits behind the Monk, who is directing Ne Zha, a heavenly deity, to fight the snakes. The waves and figures in the painting are painted with utmost care. But there is still room for improvement for their expression.

All the deities in heaven and on earth, Qing Dynasty

The Jade Emperor, supreme deity of Taoist beliefs, leads various deities in this painting. The Jade Emperor sits in the center, wearing a crown and holding an ivory tablet, with a purple aura behind him. The other deities accompany him on both sides and below him. The words on the tablet beneath the Jade Emperor mean that he is the "true ruler of all three worlds and ten directions". Two dragons are drawn above the Jade Emperor. The crowded painting has dark and strong colors.

Plowing the spring field, Qing Dynasty

This painting is aimed at urging farmers to seize the spring time to work in the fields. Four different scenes are arranged in the same painting. At the bottom, the God of Spring drives the ox to plow the field; two landlords invite a farmer to help with their work. Then there are two scenes above them: A horse gives birth to two ponies while an official announces the good harvest; three men stay near blossoming flowers and the words beside them mean “improved life”. All four scenes are connected with bumper harvest. Above the painting are the words wishing for a good harvest. The extensive use of red and yellow gives the viewer a sense of warmth and happiness. The ox and horses have flowery patterns, which is a common decoration among folk artists.

Pomegranate and peach, late Qing Dynasty

This set of paintings on young children is rather special. The children are painted in a round moon-lit circle and hold pomegranate and peach that represent multiple offspring and longevity. The peony and lotus flowers, as well as the sweet-scented osmanthus branch above the children are believed to bring good luck. The children are chubby and lovely and the woodblock printed coloring is bright.

Affluence and safety, multiple offspring, Qing Dynasty

This painting is used to decorate the window. One needs to cut it into two before putting it on. A child holds a phoenix amid flowers in a big vase. On the left vase is the Weaver Girl, a fairy who got married with the Cowherd. The vase has lotus flowers which symbolizes multiple offspring in folk legends. The right vase is painted with the Cowherd and has peony flowers that stand for affluence and safety. A pair of lions in single color are printed above the vases. This is a high quality New Year painting with well balanced structure and refined design.

Other areas

Besides the four major New Year painting production centers, other areas in the country have also formed their own distinctive styles. They can be roughly put into areas such as: Henan-Hubei, Shanxi-Shaanxi, Hunan-Anhui, Guangdong-Guangxi, Fujian-Taiwan and remote areas. Considering the influence, production era and the preservation condition of New Year paintings, this chapter has chosen some representative works from the above-mentioned areas. Limited by space, it is impossible to illustrate in detail each area's style and history. But it is hoped that the readers will be inspired to seek for more interesting samples of Chinese folk culture.

The art works chosen here feature different styles and subjects. For example, the Wuqiang New Year painting of North China's Hebei Province first appeared in the Ming Dynasty and flourished during the rules of emperors Kangxi and Qianlong of Qing Dynasty (mid-17th century to early 19th century). The paintings focus on excerpts of folk operas and feature powerful lines and striking colors made by woodblock printing. The paintings of Zhuxian Town of Central China's Henan Province also peaked in the Ming and Qing dynasties and feature stories from folk operas. Paintings from Zhuxian give more space to people than background and the woodblock printed colorful pictures are simple and full of ancient taste. The history of New Year painting production dates back much earlier in Fengxiang of Northwest China's Shaanxi Province. Some early works were made in the Song and Jin dynasties about 1,000 years ago. The paintings of door guardians are the most interesting in Fengxiang. There are more than 40 types of door guardians, all employing warm colors and exaggerated figures who wear baroque folk opera costumes. New Year paintings in North China's Shanxi Province started in the Jin Dynasty (1115-1234). The best works here are decorations on windows, some of which bear obvious influence from murals in temples. The characters are objective, with simple and unaffected coloring. The New Year paintings in Tantou of Central China's Hunan Province came from neighboring Sichuan and Guizhou provinces but established its original style at the turn of the Ming and Qing dynasties in the mid-17th century. Though the characters are simple, the coloring is brilliant and some unique painting techniques are involved. Paintings in Guangdong and Guangxi, Fujian and Taiwan, as well as the remote areas also flourished in the Qing Dynasty and feature simple colors. The religious figures and artistic effects are worthy of careful studying.

老店

Children and the heavenly officials, Qing Dynasty, Wuqiang, Hebei

This pair of paintings centers on the traditional theme of five children surrounding the heavenly official. Each child holds an auspicious item such as a lotus flower, pomegranate, colorful lantern and others. In general, such an image expresses wishes for multiple offspring and good luck. The faces of the figures are exaggerated with big eyes and pointed noses. The children and the heavenly official's clothes are painted with forceful lines. The layout structure is almost square and the block-printed colors of red, green and purple are also seldom seen.

Yellow Crane Mansion, _Dragon Matches Phoenix_, Qing Dynasty, Wuqiang, Hebei

This painting is about two stories from the *Romance of the Three Kingdoms*. The two scenes in the upper part of the painting come from the Peking Opera excerpt called *Yellow Crane Mansion* (*Huanghe Lou*). At the right, Zhou Yu hosts a banquet at the Yellow Crane Mansion and tries to force Liu Bei to give up the fertile lands of Jinzhou. At the left, general Zhao Yun breaks the bamboo and finds a secret strategy inside to save his master Liu Bei from the crisis. The two scenes below come from the opera excerpt *Dragon Matches Phoenix* (*Long Feng Pei*). At the right, Liu Bei gets married with the sister of Sun Quan; at the left, Zhao Yun escorts the newly weds back to Jinzhou. It is very difficult to inscribe so many characters with rich background on such a small painting. Each scene is marked with an explanation which shows superior technique and art level.

Weishui River, Qing Dynasty, Wuqiang, Hebei

This painting depicts the popular story of how Jiang Ziya was discovered by King Wen of Zhou Dynasty in the classic novel *Creation of the Gods*. At the top left, the woodcutter shows the way; to the right, Jiang Ziya fishes by the river. At the bottom left, King Wen of Zhou invites Jiang to his court; to the right, Jiang serves the Zhou court. It is common to see one painting containing several scenes of a story in Wuqiang works. The figures in this painting are expressive and well dressed. The coloring is dainty.

Cowherd and Weaver Girl, Qing Dynasty, Zhuxian Town, Henan

This painting is about the popular folk legend of the Cowherd and the Weaver Girl. Although details vary in different areas, this story always ends in a tragedy: The Cowherd and his fairy wife are separated by the Queen Mother of the Western Heavens. They have to stand on either side of the Milky Way and only have one chance to meet on a bridge of magpies on the night of the seventh day of the seventh lunar month. The painting features the Cowherd as holding a bamboo flute and riding on his old ox; the Weaver Girl comes in the wind. Two magpies between them are singing. The painting is rough and uninhibited with simple coloring. The figures look similar to those of Wuqiang, which shows a strong regional feature.

Shooting the bird, Qing Dynasty, Zhuxian Town, Henan

This painting comes from the folk opera *Xiao Wang Shoots the Bird*. Xiao Wang shoots a bird which falls into the garden of a rich family. The young lady of the family eventually falls in love with Xiao Wang and they get married against many odds. In the painting, Xiao Wang draws the bow, an arrow has hit the bird; two young ladies wearing long dress and holding fans are watching him with interest. This painting and the previous one both come from the Tianyi Studio of Zhuxian Town, Henan Province. The drawing is simple and unaffected.

Qin Qiong and Yuchi Gong, Qing Dynasty, Fengxiang, Shaanxi

The Tang Dynasty generals Qin Qiong and Yuchi Gong are popular door guardians. They both wear the robe with boa pattern which was designed for prince and ministers. Their weapons, the golden mace and the iron nodular staff, are decorated with red ribbon. Their faces are depicted like folk opera characters with strong personality. The costume and other ornaments are all painted with great care. The strong coloring appropriately brings out the characters' differences. This is a rare set of high quality New Year paintings.

Civil and martial Gods of Fortune, Qing Dynaty, southern Shanxi

The painting depicts the civil and martial Gods of Fortune separately. Guan Yu, a general serving Liu Bei in the Three Kingdoms Period (AD 220-280), is regarded as the Martial God of Fortune. The words above him mean that he is the only one with such great morals and martial achievements in history. The civil God of Fortune is enshrined below Guan Yu and holds the *ruyi* ornament and golden ingot. Both of them are accompanied by assistants. The characters are well designed with complicated costumes and instruments. The red and green colors create a strong visual effect.

Old Pang Wen supervises the beheading of She Taijun, Qing Dynasty, mid-Shanxi

This painting is of the same style with the previous one. It comes from a story about the fatuous emperor of Song Dynasty being cheated by the treacherous minister Pang Wen to order the killing of loyal ministers. The painting shows Pang Wen supervising the beheading of She Taijun, who was the head of the Yang Family who tried to defend the Song Dynasty from the invading Jin troops till the last drop of blood. Pang Wen sits behind a table, with a counselor standing beside him. Two sturdy guards hold glaives in front of the table. The Yang family members are seen as criminals. The painting does a fair job in depicting people of various ages and positions. The architecture is well designed.

Door guardians, Qing Dynasty, Beijing

One of the door guardians is equipped with a sword and a mace, but the other doesn't have any weapon. Thus it remains unclear who are the two guardians. Both guardians are handsome and wear different costumes featuring complicated patterns and lines. The painting has employed the traditional techniques by dyeing within golden frames. Such a high level work could have been specially commissioned by a wealthy family from famous painters.

God of Stove reports to heaven, Qing Dynasty, Beijing

This painting is about the God of Stove, who is commonly worshiped in northern China. The upper frame shows the God of Stove riding a horse to leave the Southern Heavenly Gate after reporting to the Jade Emperor. He is followed by various deities. Below, the God of Stove and his wife sit in the center, with common people celebrating the New Year. The words in the middle of the painting mean "Head of the Eastern Kitchen", "Good Luck Water" and "Kind Fire". The painting's rich content vividly depicts how the people celebrated the Spring Festival during the Qing Dynasty.

Lending the umbrella, late Qing Dynasty, Gaomi, Shandong

This painting depicts a scene from the *Tale of White Snake*. Lady White Snake lends her umbrella to the young scholar named Xu Xian. Lady Green Snake follows her elder sister. The three good-looking figures all wear splendid attire. The two young ladies' headdresses are especially interesting. The painting with simple and elegant coloring is a high-quality work from Gaomi.

Nun of Xiangshan, late Qing Dynasty, Gaomi, Shandong

The words written on the painting "*xiangshan san huanggu*" (Third Imperial Princess of Xiangshan) give a clue to the story. According to *Xiangshan Treasure Scroll* (*Xiangshan Baojuan*), the lady sitting in the painting is Miaoshan, third daughter of King Miaozhuang of the Xinglin Kingdom. Legends say that Miaoshan wanted to become a nun, but her father didn't allow her to do so. He even sent troops to kill his daughter and set fire on Xiangshan Hill, where she was seeking meditation. Later, the king fell seriously ill. Miaoshan gave up her own hands and eyes to cure her father. The figures are well painted with obvious hand-applied pigment. But the style is quite different from that of the previous work. It belongs to another period of Gaomi New Year painting.

Yuantian Emperor, modern, Lufeng, Guangdong

Yuantian Emperor, a deity in Taoism, is printed on red paper without further coloring. Of the two guardians standing beside him, the elderly guardian holds a flag and the woman holds a sword. The couplet praises the magical power of the deities. Such kind of New Year paintings is quite popular among fishermen in Guangdong.

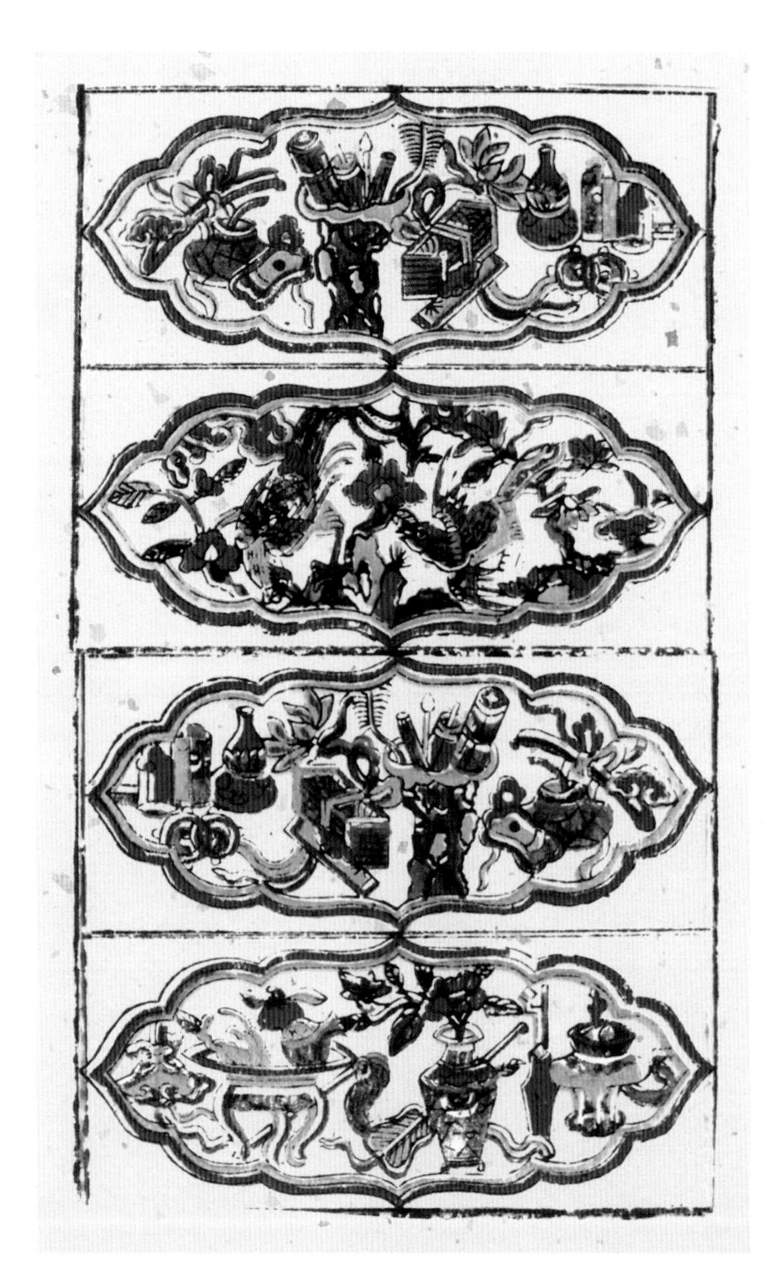

Bogu items, mid-Qing Dynasty, Zhangzhou, Fujian

The painting depicts various items used in the reading room, such as books, vase, bottle gourd, birds and flowers. Traditionally, such items are called *bogu* patterns and compose a popular theme of New Year paintings. With vivid portrayal of the items and elegant coloring, this painting is typical of such works in Zhangzhou.

Children and the door guardians, Qing Dynasty, Tantou, Hunan

This painting is about another traditional theme - five children and the door guardians. The two guardians look similar, though their faces are red and white. They wear the boa-patterned robe and hold a big axe. The five children ride the kylin animal, or hold the lotus flower and *ruyi* ornament. Obviously, the painting has been influenced by Taohuawu of Jiangsu. The words in the painting express good wishes for ample harvest. Although the characters' expressions are rigid, they are dressed brightly, carrying strong local flavor.

Big cocks, late Qing Dynasty, Linfen, Shanxi

Cock in Chinese reads as "*ji*", which is the same as "auspiciousness". Hence paintings focusing on cocks express wishes for good luck. The four cocks carry flowers of the four seasons. There are pomegranate, peach and other felicitous fruits. With dark and strong lines, the cocks have expressive eyes and the coloring is harmonious and pleasant.

Lion-Faced Tara, Qing Dynasty, Huangzhong, Qinghai

The Lion-Faced Tara is a deity worshiped in Tibetan Buddhism. She is portrayed as holding a religious instrument and a square piece of scripture decorates her chest. She steps on the lotus base in the dancing posture. In Qinghai, this kind of painting is used as door guardian. But the unique character is only seen in Qinghai and Tibet, where the Tibetans and other ethnic minorities believe in Tibetan Buddhism.

References

Deng Fuxing: *Complete Collection of Chinese Folk Art: New Year Paintings*, Jinan: Shandong Education Publishing House, Shandong Friendship Publishing House, 1995.

Wang Shuchun: *Chinese Folk New Year Paintings*, Jinan: Shandong Arts Publishing House, 1997.

Wang Shuchun: *100 Chinese Folk New Year Paintings*, Beijing: People's Arts Publishing House, 1988.

Pu Songnian: *Selection of Chinese Folk New Year Paintings*, Nanchang: Jiangxi Arts Publishing House, 1990.

Zuo Hanzhong: *Images of Woodblock Printed Folk New Year Paintings*, Changsha: Hunan Arts Publishing House, 2000.

Lan Xianlin: *Folk New Year Paintings*, Beijing: China Light Industries Publishing House, 2005.

Chen Yanqiao, Chen Qiucao, Zhu Shiji: *Folk New Year Paintings in Eastern China*, Shanghai: Shanghai People's Arts Publishing House, 1955.

Tianjin Arts Museum: *Yangliuqing New Year Paintings*, Beijing: Cultural Relics Publishing House, 1984.

Shandong Weifang Museum, Yangjiabu Woodblock New Year Paintings Research Institute: *Yangjiabu New Year Paintings*, Beijing: Cultural Relics Publishing House, 1990.

Zhang Chunfeng: *Hebei Wuqiang New Year Paintings*, Shijiazhuang: Hebei People's Publishing House, 1996.

Wang Shuchun: *Chinese Operatic New Year Paintings*, Beijing: Beijing Arts and Crafts Publishing House, 2006.

Photo sources:

Deng Fuxing: *Complete Collection of Chinese Folk Art: New Year Paintings*, Jinan: Shandong Education Publishing House, Shandong Friendship Publishing House, 1995.

Wang Shuchun: *Chinese Folk New Year Paintings*, Jinan: Shandong Arts Publishing House, 1997.